NATIVE AMERICAN HISTORIES

# THE DELAWARE

## BY MICHELLE LEVINE

CONSULTANT: JIM REMENTER
DIRECTOR, LENAPE LANGUAGE PROJECT, THE DELAWARE TRIBE OF
INDIANS, BARTLESVILLE, OKLAHOMA

LERNER PUBLICATIONS COMPANY
MINNEAPOLIS

**ABOUT THE COVER IMAGE:** The Delaware people became skilled at ribbonwork, as shown on this blanket.

PHOTO ACKNOWLEDGMENTS:

The images in this book are used with the permission of: © 2006 Harvard University, Peabody Museum Photo 99-12-10/53704 T4370.1, pp. 1, 3, 4, 13, 25, 41; © Bettmann/CORBIS, p. 5; © Tom J. Ulrich/Visuals Unlimited, p. 6; © Michael P. Gadomski/SuperStock, p. 7; © Raymond Bial, pp. 8, 18, 23, 45, 46, 47; Rare Books Division, The New York Public Library, Astor, Lenox and Tilden Foundations, p. 10; © Marilyn "Angel" Wynn/Nativestock.com, pp. 11, 16, 19, 22, 39; Illustration by John T. Kraft, Courtesy of Lenape Lifeways, Inc., pp. 12, 15, 20; © Richard Day/Daybreak Imagery, p. 14; Courtesy, National Museum of the American Indian, Smithsonian Institution (D196360b), p. 17; © MPI/Getty Images, p. 21; © North Wind Picture Archives, pp. 24, 30, 31, 33, 34, 36; Library of Congress, p. 26; © SuperStock, Inc./SuperStock, p. 27; American Swedish Historical Museum, Philadelphia, Pennsylvania, p. 28; Collection of the New-York Historical Society, 59588, p. 29; *Tishcohan* by Gustavus Hesselius, 1735. Courtesy of the Historical Society of Pennsylvania Collections, Atwater Kent Museum of Philadelphia, p. 32; © The Image Finders, p. 35; Ohio Historical Society, p. 37; Kansas State Historical Society, p. 38; "The Last Removal" by Jacob Parks, Courtesy of Jim Rementer, p. 40; Western History Collections, University of Oklahoma Library, p. 42; National Anthropological Archives, Smithsonian Institution/56938, p. 43; Jim Rementer, p. 44; © William Thomas Caine/Getty Images, p. 48; AP/Wide World Photos, p. 49. Cover: Courtesy, National Museum of the American Indian, Smithsonian Institution (D019837.000).

Text copyright ©2007 by Laura Waxman

Lerner Publications Company
A division of Lerner Publishing Group
241 First Avenue North
Minneapolis, MN 55401 U.S.A.

Website address: www.lernerbooks.com

Library of Congress Cataloging-in-Publication Data

Levine, Michelle.
    The Delaware / by Michelle Levine.
        p.    cm. — (Native American histories)
    Includes bibliographical references and index.
    ISBN-13: 978-0-8225-5914-6 (lib. bdg. : alk. paper)
    ISBN-10: 0-8225-5914-5 (lib. bdg. : alk. paper)
    1. Delaware Indians—History. 2. Delaware Indians—Government relations. 3. Delaware Indians—Social life and customs. I. Title. II. Series.
    E99.D2L465  2007
    974.004'97345—dc22                                              2005024304

Manufactured in the United States of America
1 2 3 4 5 6 – DP – 12 11 10 09 08 07

# CONTENTS

## CHAPTER 1
THE LENAPE PEOPLE............... 4

## CHAPTER 2
DAILY LIFE................. 13

## CHAPTER 3
THE COMING OF THE
WHITE MAN..................... 25

## CHAPTER 4
MODERN TIMES.................. 41

ACTIVITY .................... 50

PLACES TO VISIT ................... 52

GLOSSARY ..................... 53

FURTHER READING................. 54

WEBSITES ................... 55

SELECTED BIBLIOGRAPHY.......... 55

INDEX.................... 56

## CHAPTER 1

# THE LENAPE PEOPLE

## THE DELAWARE ARE NATIVE PEOPLE OF NORTH AMERICA.

They are often called Native Americans, or American Indians. They have lived on this continent for thousands of years. The Delaware people called themselves the Lenape (luh-NAH-pay). In their language, that word means "original people" or "common people."

Up to twenty thousand Lenape once lived in the eastern part of what later became the United States. Their homeland included modern-day New Jersey, southeastern New York, eastern Pennsylvania, and northern Delaware. This homeland is known as Lenapehoking, which means "land of the Lenape."

Many other American Indians lived near the Delaware homeland *(shown with arrow)* in eastern North America.

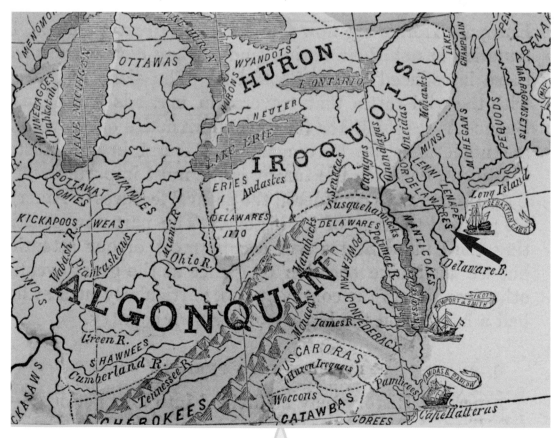

The Lenape people lived off the animals and plants in their homeland.

Green forests thick with trees and berry bushes covered Lenapehoking. The forests were home to many kinds of animals, including bears, deer, raccoons, foxes, and porcupines. Birds such as wild turkeys, geese, and ducks also lived there.

Freshwater fish filled the hundreds of rivers and streams that ran through the Lenape homeland. One of the biggest rivers was the modern-day Delaware River. In the nearby Atlantic Ocean, saltwater fish and shellfish were also common.

## LIFE IN LENAPEHOKING

Three divisions, or large groups, of Lenape probably lived in Lenapehoking. The Munsee lived in the northern part of the homeland. The Unami lived south of the Munsee. A third group, the Unalachitgo people, broke away from the Unami. Each of the three divisions had a different way of speaking the Lenape language. They also had their own ways of living. But they shared many traditions and customs.

Groups of Lenape people lived along the present-day Delaware River.

This jewelry belongs to a member of the Lenape Turtle clan.

Within each division lived members of the three main Lenape clans. A clan was made up of people who came from the same ancient family. The three clans were the Turtle, the Turkey, and the Wolf. A person was a member of his or her mother's clan. Clan members thought of one another as relatives, even if they lived far apart. People within the same clan were not allowed to marry one another.

## LENAPE VILLAGES AND HOMES

Each Lenape division was also broken up into many smaller bands. The bands lived in separate villages. These villages were independent from one another. They had their own leaders and their own rules. No one person led all the Lenape people. The village leaders were called *sakimas*. Each sakima was chosen by the people in the village.

## LENAPE WOMEN

Women played an important role in Lenape society. When two people married, the man left his home to live with the woman. The woman was considered the owner of the house and household items. Children always belonged to the mother and her clan. Women also played a leadership role. In some villages, women may have chosen the sakima.

This sketch shows sakimas Non-on-dá-gon *(right) and* Bod-a-sin *(center)* and Bod-a-sin's wife in the early 1800s.

The sakimas made decisions only with the agreement of their people. Most villages had a different leader during war. This war leader organized the village for battle. The Lenape people probably did not have a lot of battles. But different Lenape bands may have battled one another at times.

Lenape villages were usually built near rivers or streams. Land near water had the best soil for farming. Living near water also allowed people to travel from village to village by canoe.

The Lenape lived in houses with their families. Lenape men built the homes entirely from wood. They covered wooden frames with long sheets of bark. Some houses, called wigwams, were circular. Wigwams were used in the southern part of Lenapehoking.

In the northern part, most houses were long and oval with a curved roof. These longhouses usually had one door and no windows. At least one hole in the roof let out smoke from the fires below. Lenape families used fires for cooking and for heating the home in cold weather.

Lenape families lived in wigwams *(left)* and longhouses *(right)*.

Inside the longhouse, the Lenape built wooden benches and beds. They stretched animal skins across them. On the dirt floor below the benches, families often stored household items, such as pottery, baskets, dishes, and spoons. Stored food was kept cool in holes dug into the ground. Hanging from the wooden ceiling were drying herbs and ears of corn. Painted mats hung from the walls of the longhouse and lay across the benches, beds, and ground.

Sometimes, many related families shared a longhouse.

# CHAPTER 2

# DAILY LIFE

**THE LENAPE PEOPLE LIVED IN THEIR VILLAGES FOR MUCH OF THE YEAR.** But at certain times, they would leave for weeks to hunt or fish. Many kinds of animals were hunted throughout the year. Men were responsible for bringing meat and animal skins home to their family.

The Delaware often hunted birds, such as the eastern wild turkey.

In the fall, groups of people left home to hunt deer. In the winter, they hunted bears. Lenape men often hunted with bows and arrows. To catch deer or other large animals, they sometimes set fire to a part of the forest. The fire forced the animals to run to a spot where hunters were waiting. At other times, hunters formed a large circle in the forest and closed in on a group of animals.

Lenape men caught fish mostly in the spring, summer, and early fall. They often used large fishing nets. Some nets were wide enough to stretch across an entire stream. Lenape also traveled to the coast to catch shellfish and sea fish from the ocean. They used canoes dug out of tree trunks to travel from place to place.

The hunters and fishers were careful to kill only as many animals as their families needed to survive. They gave thanks for the lives of the animals. They also tried not to waste any part of the animals.

Lenape fishers used huge nets to trap small fish called shad. Then they speared the fish or caught them with their hands.

The Lenape laid strips of meat on sticks over a fire.
The smoke from the fire dried the meat and kept flies away from it.

## WOMEN'S WORK

Back at home, the women cleaned and cooked meat from the fish and other animals. They dried any extra meat. To dry the meat, women cut it into thin strips. Then they smoked the strips over a fire. The dried meat could be stored. The Lenape ate it in the winter when hunting was difficult.

Women also cleaned and prepared the skins of deer and other animals. They sewed the skins into blankets, sacks, and clothing. Lenape women often wore deerskin skirts. The men wore breechcloths. A breechcloth is a long piece of deerskin that goes between the legs and is kept on by a belt. In the colder months, men and women put on leggings and soft leather shoes called moccasins. They also wore fur robes and beautiful cloaks made of bird feathers.

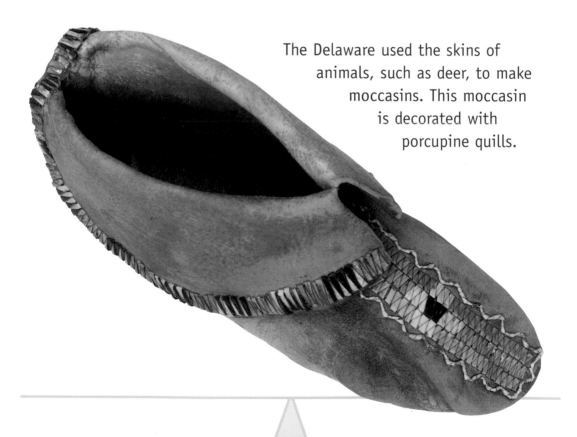

The Delaware used the skins of animals, such as deer, to make moccasins. This moccasin is decorated with porcupine quills.

The Lenape found uses for other animal parts too. Claws became part of jewelry. Porcupine quills were dyed and sewn into colorful patterns on clothing. Shells from shellfish also decorated clothing and were worn as jewelry. The Lenape even used the fat from bears to keep their hair and skin healthy. The fat also kept insects from biting them.

Some Lenape hunters wore bear claw necklaces as a sign of their strength and skill.

Delaware women had many ways to prepare corn, squash, and beans to feed their families.

Along with cooking and making clothing, women grew and harvested crops. They planted corn, beans, and squash in fields near their villages. Corn was an especially useful crop. Women boiled cobs of corn in pots over the fire. They also dried the corn and pounded it into flour. They used the flour to make flatbreads and other foods. It was also a woman's job to gather nuts, berries, herbs, and firewood from the forest.

# THE CREATION OF EARTH

One well-known Lenape creation story says that in the beginning there was no Earth, only the sea. One day, the first human being fell from the heavens above into the sea. A sea turtle living deep below the ocean took pity on this woman. The turtle rose up and let the woman rest on its shell. Land began to form around the turtle's back *(left)*. This land became Earth. Then the woman gave birth to two children and to the animals of Earth.

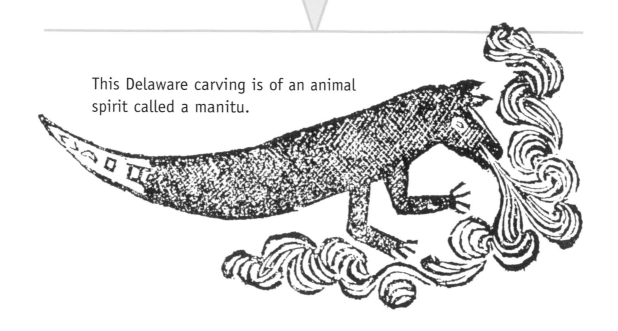

This Delaware carving is of an animal spirit called a manitu.

## LENAPE SPIRITUAL BELIEFS

According to a Lenape legend, the Lenape believed in one god, the Creator. The Creator lived up in the highest heaven. Below the Creator were eleven other heavens. And below those heavens was Earth. Everything on Earth was alive with a manitu, a spirit being made by the Creator.

Each animal, from the smallest insect to the great black bear, had its own manitu. Even rocks and trees had manitus. The sun, moon, and wind were also spirit beings. The Lenape always tried to live in harmony with nature. They did not want to offend any manitu by treating an animal, plant, or other part of nature poorly.

Some manitus were more powerful than others. One spirit was called the Masked Being, Living Solid Face, and other names. He protected deer and other large animals. The Lenape believed this manitu could cause a person to succeed or fail in hunting. To honor this spirit, the Lenape made a sacred mask in his image. Lenape people used the mask in ceremonies.

To send their prayers to a manitu or to the Creator, the Lenape often smoked a pipe. For the most sincere prayers, they burned leaves from a cedar tree. The Lenape believed the smoke rising to the sky helped their prayers reach the heavens.

This is a Masked Being mask. Half of it is painted red. The other half is painted black.

During a vision quest, a Delaware boy went to a quiet spot and waited to hear from his guardian spirit. This spirit was often a bird or other animal.

For boys, an important ceremony was the vision quest. During a vision quest, a boy discovered the identity of his guardian spirit. Around the age of twelve to fifteen, a boy went deep into the woods alone. Sometimes he went to a mountaintop or another place without people. During this time, he did not eat any food. He offered prayers and waited for a voice or vision. Once he heard a voice or saw a vision, the boy would know who his guardian spirit was. From then on, he relied on this spirit to guide him through life.

Sometimes a Lenape person would also seek the guidance of a medicine man or woman. These spiritual healers used special prayers and medicines from plants to cure illnesses or other problems. People also went to such healers to seek better luck in farming, hunting, love, or other parts of their lives.

Lenape medicine men and women danced while they prayed for their patients.

## CHAPTER 3

# THE COMING OF THE WHITE MAN

**THE FIRST EUROPEAN KNOWN TO COME TO THE LENAPE HOMELAND** was Giovanni da Verrazano. This Italian explorer sailed along the coast of Lenapehoking in 1524. In 1609, an English explorer named Henry Hudson also came across some Lenape Indians.

Native Americans living on the East Coast of North America watch a European ship approach them in the 1600s. Europeans came to Lenape land about this time.

After that, people from Europe began living on parts of Lenape land. These white men noticed that many Lenape people lived along a large river that a European had named the Delaware River. The Europeans began calling the Lenape the Delaware people.

## LIVING WITH THE EUROPEANS

Many Europeans who came to North America in the 1600s were interested in hunting and trapping animals for their fur. Clothing made of fur was very popular in Europe. The hunters and trappers traded European goods for fur from Lenape hunters. For the first time, the Lenape people had metal tools, such as axes and knifes. They also bought guns, glass beads, and cloth from the Europeans.

In the 1600s, many Native Americans also traded corn for European goods.

More and more Europeans crossed the ocean.
They needed land, and the Lenape agreed to sell
some. But the Lenape and the Europeans had a
different idea of what it meant to sell land. The
Lenape believed that land was like air, water,
and sunlight. It could not be owned, only shared.
The Lenape people thought the white men were
paying them to share their land for a while. The
Europeans who bought the land believed it was
theirs to keep.

Settlers from Sweden first landed in North America in 1638.

Dutch settlers also began settling on Delaware lands. They set up ports and towns, such as New Amsterdam *(above)*. The British took it over in 1664 and renamed it New York.

Along with losing some of their land, the Lenape lost many loved ones. The Europeans brought with them deadly diseases, such as smallpox. These diseases spread quickly among Lenape villages. Over time, thousands of Lenape died. People lost their children, parents, brothers, and sisters. In some villages, almost everyone died.

Life became even more difficult for the Lenape people after 1664. That year, the British took over the land claimed by other Europeans. The British wanted to settle the land and create permanent colonies.

White settlers harvested crops in their fields along the Delaware River.

The colonists began clearing forests for farms and homes. They let their farm animals roam free and eat the crops of nearby Lenape farms and gardens. Hunting was also more difficult. Both white and Indian hunters had killed too many animals for their fur. That left the Lenape with barely enough animals to hunt for food.

## MOVING WEST

The British were destroying life as the Lenape had known it. Meanwhile, many Lenape people had become dependent on European goods such as tools and guns. But land was all many Lenape had to sell.

Many Lenape people gave up their homelands to the British and moved west. They ended up in Pennsylvania. A British Quaker named William Penn started the colony of Pennsylvania in 1682. Members of the Quaker religion believed in living peacefully and treating people fairly. Penn wanted to buy land from the Lenape. But he tried to treat them better than other Europeans had.

The Lenape leader Tamanend presented a wampum belt *(detail, below)* to William Penn in 1682. This belt of shell pieces marked the treaty Penn made with the Lenape people in Pennsylvania.

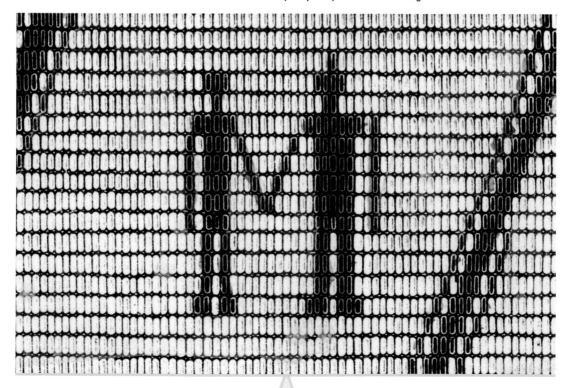

After William Penn died, his sons took over running the colony. They did not care about treating the Lenape fairly. In 1737, Penn's sons cheated the Lenape out of most of their land. They used a false treaty. The sons told the Lenape people that past Lenape leaders had signed this written agreement. In it, the Lenape people promised to sell as much land as a person could walk in a day and a half. This agreement later became known as the Walking Purchase.

Tishcohan (left) and other Lenape leaders signed the 1737 treaty with William Penn's sons.

The Walking Purchase cheated the Lenape people out of most of their land in Pennsylvania. This painting shows the white walkers with two American Indians.

The Lenape figured that a person could only walk through part of their land in a day and a half. But Penn's sons secretly hired men to clear paths through the forest. Then they hired runners to race along these paths as fast as they could. The men ran through almost all of the Lenape land in a day and half. Once again, the Lenape were forced to move farther west. Many settled in modern-day Ohio.

## FROM THE BRITISH TO THE AMERICANS

In the late 1700s, the Lenape and other American Indians got caught up in the American Revolution (1775–1783). American colonists were fighting British soldiers for the right to rule their own country. Some Lenape sided with the Americans. Some sided with the British. Others stayed out of the fighting altogether.

Sometimes soldiers in the American Revolution attacked Native American villages.

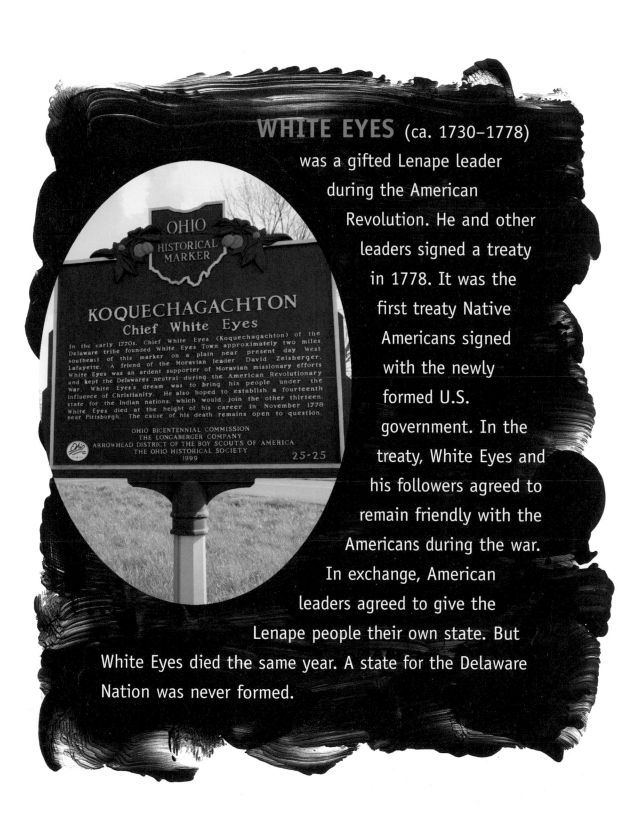

**WHITE EYES** (ca. 1730–1778) was a gifted Lenape leader during the American Revolution. He and other leaders signed a treaty in 1778. It was the first treaty Native Americans signed with the newly formed U.S. government. In the treaty, White Eyes and his followers agreed to remain friendly with the Americans during the war. In exchange, American leaders agreed to give the Lenape people their own state. But White Eyes died the same year. A state for the Delaware Nation was never formed.

The historical marker reads:

**OHIO**
**HISTORICAL MARKER**

**KOQUECHAGACHTON**
Chief White Eyes

In the early 1770s, Chief White Eyes (Koquechagachton) of the Delaware tribe founded White Eyes Town approximately two miles southeast of this marker on a plain near present day West Lafayette. A friend of the Moravian leader David Zeisberger, White Eyes was an ardent supporter of Moravian missionary efforts and kept the Delawares neutral during the American Revolutionary War. White Eyes's dream was to bring his people under the influence of Christianity. He also hoped to establish a fourteenth state for the Indian nations, which would join the other thirteen. White Eyes died at the height of his career in November 1778 near Pittsburgh. The cause of his death remains open to question.

OHIO BICENTENNIAL COMMISSION
THE LONGABERGER COMPANY
ARROWHEAD DISTRICT OF THE BOY SCOUTS OF AMERICA
THE OHIO HISTORICAL SOCIETY
1999

25-25

American soldiers did not always understand
which Indians were their friends during the war. In
1782, a group of Americans attacked a town in Ohio
called Gnadenhutten. It was founded by the
Moravian (Christian) church. The Americans killed
nearly one hundred Lenape men, women, and
children here. The killing became known as the
Gnadenhutten massacre. This unfair treatment
saddened and angered the Lenape people.

Americans accused Moravian Lenape in Gnadenhutten of
taking part in raids against Americans. The Americans killed
the Lenape and burned down all the buildings.

The Lenape and other Native Americans signed
the Treaty of Greenville in 1795.

The United States won the war in 1783. The new
government wanted to take over Lenape land in
Ohio. The Lenape decided to fight for the land with
help from an army of other Native Americans. The
U.S. government sent many soldiers to battle the
American Indian warriors. The U.S. soldiers had
more fighters and better weapons. By 1795, the
Native Americans gave up fighting. They agreed to
leave their land. Many Lenape were forced to move
into western Ohio and Indiana. Others ended up in
Canada, Wisconsin, Michigan, Missouri, Arkansas,
and Texas.

In the 1800s, the United States began to settle on land farther and farther west. The U.S. government forced the Lenape and many other Native Americans to places west of the Mississippi River. Most Lenape made this long journey between 1820 and 1821. The Lenape did not have proper clothing or food for the journey. Many young children and older people died.

Anna Marshall Grinter *(left)* was a Lenape woman born in Ohio in 1820. Her Lenape name was Windagamen. In just ten years, her family moved from Ohio to Indiana to Missouri and finally to Kansas.

# THE BIG HOUSE

The Lenape struggled to keep their traditions alive after the Europeans and Americans took over their land. Wherever they went, the Lenape built a special building called the Big House. It was a large cabin made of wood. Inside was a center post with carvings on it. The Lenape believed the post connected the heavens with Earth. The four walls faced the four directions. Once a year, people gathered for twelve days for the Big House Ceremony. They gave thanks to the Creator and the manitus for all that was good. Men shared their visions and spiritual dreams. The last Big House Ceremony took place in Oklahoma in 1924.

These drumsticks were used in the Big House Ceremony. A frowning face is carved on each stick and painted red.

The Lenape who survived settled in Missouri.
This land turned out to be terrible for farming.
The Lenape asked the U.S. government for better
land. After eight years, the government agreed to
give the Lenape territory in Kansas. Lenape
families built homes and started new farms there.
They lived in peace for years. Then their lives
changed. White settlers wanted to move to
Kansas. By the 1860s, the Lenape no longer felt
safe there. It was time to move west again.

A Lenape named Jacob Parks (1890–1949) painted this scene
of a Delaware family leaving their Kansas home in 1867.

THE LAST REMOVAL

## CHAPTER 4

# MODERN TIMES

**IN THE LATE 1860s, MANY LENAPE PEOPLE MOVED TO MODERN-DAY OKLAHOMA.**
Cherokee Indians already lived on much of this land. They had agreed to sell some land to the Lenape people in a treaty. The Lenape who moved to Oklahoma struggled to keep their history and traditions alive. But as older people died, their memories of the past died with them.

Lenape women practice sewing at an Oklahoma mission in 1898. White people set up these church schools to teach Native Americans about the Christian religion and white ways of living.

Life became harder when Oklahoma became a state in 1907. The U.S. government took over the Cherokee and Lenape lands and leadership. The government also forced many children of the Lenape and other Native Americans into boarding schools. In these schools, children were punished for speaking their traditional languages or practicing their beliefs.

By the 1950s, many Lenape people had lost touch with their past. Few of them still spoke or understood the traditional language. Many no longer practiced or remembered old Lenape customs or beliefs. Many younger Lenape thought their grandparents and great-grandparents had always lived in the West. Some people feared that the Lenape ways of life were gone forever.

Lenape families made this kind of doll for the yearly Doll Dance. By the mid-1900s, many Lenape had only objects such as this to connect them to their traditions. But few remembered why the objects were important.

The traditional Lenape healer Nora Thompson Dean *(left)* also went by the name Touching Leaves Woman. As a child, she saw the Big House Ceremony and many Lenape traditions.

## REMEMBERING OLD WAYS

One woman helped her people remember their past. Her name was Nora Thompson Dean. By the 1960s, Dean was one of the few Lenape who still spoke her people's language. She also had great knowledge of ancient Lenape traditions. Dean worked with Lenape people and others who were interested in learning about Lenape culture. She gave talks and workshops and led ceremonies. Since her death in 1984, other Lenape have carried on her work. They keep the Lenape language, traditions, and memories alive.

## MODERN-DAY LENAPE

Modern Lenape people live in towns and cities all across the United States. Most Lenape live in Oklahoma. Lenape also live in Ontario, Canada. Many Lenape families live among white neighbors. Like their neighbors, they live in modern homes and wear modern clothing. Lenape men and women have many kinds of jobs. They work in places such as schools, hospitals, businesses, farms, and factories.

This is the Delaware Tribal Community Center and Child Care building in Bartlesville, Oklahoma.

These women are wearing modern clothing with Lenape designs.

Many Lenape people are interested in learning about and celebrating their traditions. In states such as Oklahoma, Indiana, and Pennsylvania, Lenape gather each year for a powwow. At this Native American gathering, Lenape people celebrate their culture. Some of them wear traditional clothing and take part in old dances. They play traditional music and tell ancient Lenape stories.

A group of Lenape in Oklahoma celebrate Delaware Day each year. This day gives Lenape families a chance to come together and learn about their history and culture. Children play traditional games. Ceremonial dances and Lenape football are also popular parts of this event.

For the Gourd Dance, Lenape men hold rattles in their right hands and feather fans in their left hands.

In Wilmington, Delaware, two Lenape people in traditional dress teach Crown Princess Victoria of Sweden *(center)* and others traditional dance steps.

A smaller number of Lenape live in the old homeland, Lenapehoking. These Lenape also honor their past. A traditional Lenape village has been re-created in Waterloo, New Jersey. Here visitors can see Lenape homes, crops, games, and masks as they were in the past.

The Lenape people in Canada have also found ways to celebrate their old ways of life. They host powwows like the ones in the United States. In 1992, they celebrated the Fall Gathering. Lenape from across Canada took part in traditional ceremonies, prayers, meals, and deer hunts.

## LOST LANDS

In recent years, Lenape people in Oklahoma have worked together to win payments for their lost land. In the mid-1970s, they took their case to court. The courts made the U.S. government pay the Lenape people $9 million for land it took years ago. In the 2000s, some Oklahoma Lenape *(below)* continued to take their case to court. They hoped that some of the Walking Purchase land would be returned to them.

The Lenape people nearly lost their culture and history. They have many reasons to celebrate their past. Through storytelling and teaching, they are keeping their traditions strong for many years to come.

# PAHSAHËMAN (LENAPE FOOTBALL)

This traditional Lenape game is most often played between men and women. The players use an oval-shaped ball made of deerskin stuffed with hair. A football or soccer ball may also be used.

## TEAMS:

Boys and girls are divided into two separate teams. The two teams can be of any size.

## PLAYING FIELD:

Each team has a goal on either side of the field. Traditionally, the goal is made of two goalposts about six feet (two meters) apart. The space between the posts is the goal. The goalposts can be trees or actual posts stuck into the ground. A rope or other material can also be placed on the ground to make a six-foot (two-meter) line marking each team's goal.

## RULES:

Girls and boys follow different rules. To pass the ball or make a goal, girls can carry the ball, run with it, throw it, or kick it. Boys cannot carry, run with, or throw the ball. If they catch the ball or get it from another player, they can kick it toward the goal or to another team member. Both boys and girls can try to block one another from getting to their team's goal, but they should not grab or tackle one another.

## BEGINNING THE GAME:

The game begins when the scorekeeper stands in the middle of the field and throws the ball in the air. Each team tries to get the ball.

## SCORING:

A point is scored each time a team member gets the ball through the other team's goal. An adult or child not playing the game should be in charge of keeping score. The score is kept using twelve sticks. Each time a team wins a point, the scorekeeper puts one stick in a pile for that team.

## ENDING THE GAME:

The game ends when all the sticks have been used up. Then the sticks are counted. The team with the most sticks wins the game. If the score is tied, 6 to 6, a play-off takes place until one more goal is made.

# PLACES TO VISIT

### Conner Prairie

*Fishers, Indiana*
(317) 776-6006
http://connerprairie.org/planyourvisit/lenape.aspx
Visitors to this outdoor history museum can experience what life was like in an 1816 Lenape camp.

### National Museum of the American Indian

*Washington, D. C.*
(202) 633-1000
http://www.nmai.si.edu
Part of the Smithsonian Institution, this museum allows visitors to explore Native American life and history. Works of many Native American artists and craftspeople are also featured.

### Schoenbrunn Village

*Zoar, Ohio*
(330) 339-3636
http://www.ohiohistory.org/places/schoenbr
This reconstructed village resembles the mission town of Schoenbrunn. The Moravian church founded Schoenbrunn for Christian Delaware in the 1770s.

### Waterloo Village

*Stanhope, New Jersey*
(973) 347-0900
http://www.waterloovillage.org
At this living history museum, a traditional Lenape village has been re-created. Visitors to the village are able to see the way Lenape people may have lived before the time of the Europeans.

# GLOSSARY

**band:** a group of Lenape living together, usually in a village

**clan:** a large group of families sharing a common ancestor through the mother's side. Lenape society was separated into three clans.

**colony:** a group of people who settle far from home but maintain ties to their homeland

**division:** a large group of people. The Lenape were broken up into three main divisions: the Munsee, the Unami, and the Unalachitgo.

**Lenapehoking:** a Lenape word meaning "land of the Lenape." It refers to the traditional eastern homeland of the Lenape people.

**longhouse:** a long oval house the Lenape people made of wood

**manitu:** a spirit being made by the Creator

**native:** originally from a place. The Lenape are native to North America.

**powwow:** a Native American gathering

**Quaker:** a member of the Quaker religion, which encourages people to live peacefully and treat others with respect

**sakima:** Lenape leader or chief

**treaty:** a written agreement between two or more nations or groups

**wigwam:** a circular house made of wood and bark. These Lenape homes were used in the southern part of the Lenape people's traditional homeland.

# FURTHER READING

Bierhorst, John. ed. *The White Deer and Other Stories Told by the Lenape*. New York: William Morrow and Co., 1995. Various Lenape people share traditional Lenape stories in this book.

Durrant, Lynda. *Beaded Moccasins: The Story of Mary Campbell*. New York: Dell Yearling, 2000. This novel is based on the true story of twelve-year-old Mary Campbell, who was kidnapped by Lenape Indians in 1759 and came to embrace her new way of life.

Johnston, Norma. *Feather in the Wind*. New York: Marshall Cavendish, 2001. In this novel, fourteen-year-old Becca Standish moves from Switzerland to her family's old home in New Jersey, where she encounters the ghost of a Lenape boy from the 1700s.

Keehn, Sally M. *Moon of Two Dark Horses*. New York: Philomel Books, 1995. Twelve-year-old Coshmoo, a Lenape boy, and his white settler friend, Daniel, try to keep bloodshed away from their home and prevent the Lenape from losing more of their land during the American Revolution.

Osborne, Mary Pope. *Standing in the Light: The Captive Diary of Catharine Carey Logan, Delaware Valley, Pennsylvania, 1763*. New York: Scholastic, Inc., 1998. Part of the Dear America series, this is the fictional story of a thirteen-year-old Quaker girl living in Pennsylvania who is captured and then cared for by Lenape Indians in 1763.

Wilker, Josh. *The Lenape Indians*. New York: Chelsea Juniors, 1994. The author gives a description of Lenape culture and history.

# WEBSITES

**Delaware (Lenape) Tribe of Indians**
http://www.delawaretribeofindians.nsn.us/
Created by a tribe of Lenape living in Oklahoma, this website has links to information about Lenape history, culture, language, and modern life.

**Touching Leaves Woman (Nora Thompson Dean)**
http://www.nationwide.net/~david/artists/oestreicher/
touchingleaveswoman.html
This Web page has information about the woman who helped keep Lenape culture, traditions, and language alive in modern times.

# SELECTED BIBLIOGRAPHY

Bierhorst, John, ed. *Mythology of the Lenape: Guide and Texts*. Tucson: University of Arizona Press, 1995.

———. *The White Deer and Other Stories Told by the Lenape*. New York: William Morrow and Co., 1995.

Dowd, Gregory Evans. *The Indians of New Jersey*. Trenton: New Jersey Historical Commission, Department of State, 1992.

Kraft, Herbert C. *The Lenape-Delaware Indian Heritage: 10,000 B.C.–A.D. 2000*. Stanhope, NJ: Lenape Lifeways, Inc., 2001.

Weslager, C. A. *The Delaware Indians: A History*. New Brunswick, NJ: Rutgers University Press, 1972.

# INDEX

American Revolution, 34–39
animals, 6, 8, 13–18, 20, 21, 22, 23, 27, 30

beliefs and legends, 20–24, 39, 42, 43
Big House, 39, 44
British, 29–31, 34

ceremonies, 22–23, 39, 43, 44, 46–47, 48
clans, 8, 9
clothing, 17–18, 45, 46, 49
creation story, 20

Dean, Nora Thompson, 44
Delaware River, 6, 7, 26
diseases, 29
divisions, 7–9

Europeans, 25–31, 39

farming, 19, 24, 40
fishing, 13, 15
food, 12, 13–16, 19, 30

gathering, 19

homeland, 5–7, 25, 48
homes, 11–12, 45, 48
Hudson, Henry, 25

hunting, 13–14, 15, 18, 22, 24, 27, 30

land ownership, 28–29, 30–32, 40–42, 49
language, 4, 7, 42, 43, 44
leadership, 9–10, 31, 32, 35, 42
Lenape football, 47, 50–51

manitus, 21–22, 39
medicine men and women, 24, 44
moving west, 31, 33, 37–38, 40

names, 4, 26

Penn, William, 31–32

schools and education, 42

Tamanend, 31
trade, 27, 30
treaties, 31, 32–33, 35, 37, 41

villages, 9–10, 13, 29, 34

Walking Purchase, 32–33
war and warriors, 10, 34–37
White Eyes, 35
women, 9, 16–17, 19